KISS ME LIKE YOU MEAN IT

Chris Chibnall

KISS ME LIKE YOU MEAN IT

OBERON BOOKS
LONDON

First published in 2001 by Oberon Books Ltd.
521 Caledonian Road, London N7 9RH
Tel: +44 (0) 20 7607 3637 / Fax: +44 (0) 20 7607 3629
e-mail: info@oberonbooks.com
www.oberonbooks.com

A catalogue record for this book is available from the British
Library.

PB ISBN: 9781840022360
E ISBN: 9781849435642

Cover design by James Illman

Acknowledgements

No play is an island. I'd like to thank those without whom…

Huge thanks go to: Abigail Morris, Paul Sirett, Mark Brickman, Lin Coghlan, Sara Murray, James Rose, Matthew Broughton, Madeline Joinson, Cathy King & Phil Temple, the five other Soho-attached writers (John, Holly, Trevor, Marta and Suzy), Lee Ingleby, Keeley Forsyth, Collette O'Neil, Tony Rohr, all at GriP Theatre (Nigel, Becky, Kat, Sanchia, Michael) and, of course, the cast at Soho: Jason, Catherine, Marlene and Harry.

Finally, a special note of love and thanks to Martin & Chantal Richards for finding and putting me on the road here.

The text is accurate to the end of the second week of rehearsal.

for Maddie and for Bomps

Characters

RUTH
a girl in her twenties

TONY
a boy in his twenties

EDIE
a woman in her late sixties/early seventies

DON
a man in his late sixties/early seventies

Author's Note

Trashy modern party music plays as the audience comes in:

Dancing In The Moonlight by Toploader
Stuck In A Moment You Can't Get Out Of by U2
Would You? by Touch and Go
She Bangs by Ricky Martin
Mambo Number 5 by Lou Bega

– that sort of thing.

Kiss Me Like You Mean It was first performed at Soho Theatre and Writers' Centre on 21 May 2001, with the following cast:

TONY, Jason Hughes

RUTH, Catherine McCormack

EDIE, Marlene Sidaway

DON, Harry Towb

Director, Abigail Morris

Designer, Will Hargreaves

ACT ONE

'Sex Bomb' by Tom Jones and Mousse T crashes in through the darkness. After a few seconds, lights come up on stage.

Manchester. Present day. 3 am. A clear, hot summer's night/early morning.

The back garden of a large, rather shabby Victorian terrace house. The tail end of a party in progress inside. The back door is open. The music belts out.

TONY slides fast into the doorway. He's twenty-five, happy and enthusiastic. He sings and dances down the steps – his own drunken sex-god choreography.

After a few moments of TONY's dancing, RUTH appears in fast pursuit. She is twenty-six, strong and sexy. She calls after him.

RUTH: (*Trying to be heard over the music.*) Oy!

TONY is oblivious. He's on Top of the Pops. In his head.

Oy, you!

TONY gears up for a big finish to the song. He still has his back to RUTH.

(*Shouting.*) Hey! Ricky Martin!

TONY still oblivious.

(*Yelling at the top of her voice.*) That's my bloody drink, shitforbrains!

TONY: Look, what's the –

He turns. Clocks RUTH for the first time. Freezes. He looks at RUTH, gobsmacked. He is wowed; still completing the previous sentence.

– problem?

9

RUTH: You've nicked my bloody beer, that's the problem, pal!

TONY: Did I?

RUTH: Yeah!

TONY: Oh.

RUTH: So?

TONY: So. What?

RUTH: Can I have it back?

TONY: Oh! Yes. Sorry. (*He hands it back.*) It was on the side, see.

RUTH: Yeah. Next to me.

TONY: I didn't see you.

RUTH: Apparently.

TONY: We brought some of those with us.

RUTH: Yeah – four cans.

TONY: Yeah. Probably about that.

RUTH: We brought a crate.

TONY: Oh.

He grins at RUTH. His best girl-pulling grin. It's not too effective.

RUTH: Got a fag?

TONY: (*Shaking his head.*) No. (*Sudden panic.*) I mean, yes! *Not* no! Yes! To clarify. Yes.

RUTH: Can I have one?

TONY: What? Oh! Yeah! Sure. Fag. Yes. Fag. Course. Fag.

TONY taps his body for the packet. Eventually fishes a bat-

tered pack of Marlboro Lights out of his pocket. He offers RUTH a cigarette.

RUTH smiles her gratitude and takes one. Puts it in her mouth.

TONY looks at her. Smiles awkwardly. They both stand there.

RUTH: Light?

TONY: (*Awakened from his reverie.*) Yeah!

He reaches back in his pocket and pulls out a Gold Zippo. He flashes it at RUTH and waits half a second for her to be impressed. Nothing. TONY clicks his fingers over the top of the lighter to open the lid. It works. He thinks he's George Clooney in 'Out of Sight'. He goes for the second move. He clicks his fingers over the Zippo to light it. Having done this, he smiles at RUTH, coolly.

RUTH returns the smile – weakly. The Zippo has not lit.

Shit.

TONY tries the Zippo trick again. Nothing. Shamed, he tries to light it in the more pedestrian, normal fashion. Nothing – a spark, but no flame. Frustration. TONY shakes the lighter. Tries to light it again. Still nothing. He tries a few more times, getting more and more annoyed.

After a bit, RUTH can bear it no longer. TONY is fiddling.

RUTH: (*Leaning over the lighter.*) Here let me –

TONY: (*Talking over her.*) No wait, I think I've –

TONY flicks the lighter. It shoots out a massive, high jet of flame, nearly burning RUTH's face off.

RUTH jumps back, trying to avoid death.

RUTH: FOR CHRIST'S SAKE!!!!

TONY: (*At the same time.*) BLOODY HELL!

RUTH: (*Annoyed.*) You trying to kill me?!!?!

TONY: Sorry, sorry!

TONY lights the Zippo again, more cautiously. It is normal. He holds it out to RUTH.

RUTH approaches it gingerly and takes a light off the flame, before stepping back.

They stand, a few feet apart. Smoking. Not saying anything.

Stupid lighter.

RUTH smiles and nods patronisingly.

It was a bargain, though.

RUTH: I wonder why.

Silent smoking returns. TONY is desperate to pick up the reins.

TONY: Been a good party!

RUTH: D'you think so?

TONY: Yeah! Don't you?

RUTH: I think it's been shit.

TONY: Yeah. Shit.

He nods vociferously. They smoke.

Tony.

RUTH: Eh?

TONY: Tony.

RUTH: I see.

More smoking.

Ruth.

TONY: Ruth?

RUTH: (*Nods.*) Ruth.

TONY: Welsh?

RUTH: No.

TONY: Oh.

RUTH: Why?

TONY: Because I thought maybe I don't know actually
I have no idea.

RUTH: Hmm.

TONY: The Welsh woman on *Hi-de-Hi* was Ruth.

RUTH: What?

TONY: Nothing.

More smoking.

So how d'you know Brian then?

RUTH: Brian?

TONY: It's his party.

RUTH: I don't.

TONY: So how come you're here then?

RUTH: I know Amanda.

TONY: Which one's Amanda?

RUTH: Jackie's best mate.

TONY: Who's Jackie?

RUTH: Goes out with Mike.

TONY: Mike?

RUTH: Fiona's ex.

TONY: Don't know Fiona.

RUTH: Shagged Clark at Rachel's birthday

TONY: Hang on, who's Rachel? Who's Clark?

RUTH: Jesus, d'you know anyone?

TONY: I thought I did.

RUTH: I mean, what you doing here if you know nobody?

TONY: Brian's me best mate.

RUTH: Oh.

TONY: So...here with your...

TONY makes obscure gestures with his hands to avoid using a particular word.

– you're not gay, are you?

RUTH: What?

TONY: (*Defensive.*) Some people are!

RUTH: Not gay. Not Welsh. Okay?

TONY: Right. So you're here with your...

RUTH: Boyfriend.

TONY: Boyfriend.

RUTH: Yeah.

TONY: Oh.

RUTH: He's inside.

TONY: Right. Big fella?

RUTH: Rugby player.

TONY: Oh. How long you been seeing each other?

RUTH: What is this, *Fifteen to One*?

TONY: Just talking.

RUTH: Five years.

TONY: Serious then.

RUTH: If you like.

TONY: Five years. Wow. You must really be… Get along… Well.

RUTH sighs.

RUTH: Well, thanks for my drink back. And, er, I wouldn't take up dancing full time.

TONY: Where are you going?

RUTH: Inside.

TONY: But –

RUTH: But what?

TONY: We've only just –

RUTH: – what? –

TONY: – well –

RUTH: – what?!? –

TONY: – you know –

RUTH: – no! –

TONY: – started.

RUTH: Started? What d'you mean started?

TONY: Met. Begun.

RUTH: Begun!

TONY: What?

RUTH: I'm going inside.

TONY: No, don't you see –

RUTH: My idiot alert is going thirteen to the dozen here.

TONY: Come on. Ruth. We're only talking.

RUTH: Is that what you call it?

TONY: I'm not a nutter. Promise. Just stay and have a chat eh? What harm's it gonna do?

RUTH: I've a boyfriend inside.

TONY: Of course.

RUTH breathes out. She shakes her head.

TONY looks at her hopefully, smiling.

RUTH goes up the steps and inside.

TONY stands and watches her go. He moves to get a different angle on the door, peering up at it, expecting RUTH to appear again. He stands alone. Crumples his beer can.

Shit.

He looks back again. Still nothing.

Shit shit shit shit and shit.

TONY paces.

Dear Robert Kilroy Silk. Have you ever considered doing a programme called *I Can't Stop Talking Bollocks To Women*. I think it would be a winner and would be more than happy to share my own extensive experiences with your viewers.

He sighs.

The sound of someone singing upstairs. They are singing the tune to 'The Stripper'.

EDIE'S VOICE: Da da da, da-da da da
Da da da, da DA da da-da...

TONY looks up.

An old woman's bottom is clearly visible in the window. It's wearing some particularly fine underwear.

EDIE – a woman in her early seventies – is performing a flamboyant striptease, in silhouette. She's really enjoying herself. She ends up wiggling her bum in the window.

TONY watches open-mouthed.

RUTH appears and descends the stairs clasping a couple of cans.

RUTH: That whole bloody crate's been gone through! Honestly, people are bastards. (*She notices TONY's wide-eyed expression.*) What's up with you?

TONY: Look!

He points up to the window. The bum is no longer there. RUTH follows his pointing.

RUTH: Ooh. A window.

TONY: No, there was a – (*He tries a haphazard mime.*)

RUTH: A what?

TONY: Well – (*Another mime.*)

RUTH: How many syllables?

TONY: An arse!

RUTH: Same to you.

TONY: (*Despairing.*) There was an old woman's arse up there!

RUTH: Just an arse? Or was there anyone attached to it?

TONY: I couldn't see.

RUTH: Maybe you've had enough beer.

TONY: You don't believe me?

RUTH: It's three am pal. Not exactly prime time for pensioner sex frenzies.

TONY: It was definitely there.

RUTH: Have a drink and shut up.

TONY: Cheers.

RUTH opens her can of beer.

TONY opens his can. It explodes all over him, drenching him. He looks at RUTH.

Was that you?

RUTH: (*All innocence.*) What?

TONY: This is my best shirt!

RUTH: I wouldn't boast about it.

TONY wipes down his shirt.

TONY: You came back then.

RUTH: No. I'm still inside.

TONY: Right.

RUTH: Half the place is crashed out now. You're one of the few conscious options.

TONY: Thanks very much.

He finishes wiping the shirt. Cleans his hands on his trousers.

Tony.

RUTH: Eh?

TONY: Do it properly this time. Don't be arsey.

RUTH: Who said I was –

TONY: (*Insistently.*) Tony. How d'you do.

RUTH: Ruth. Charmed, I'm sure.

TONY: Lovely.

They both look out.

Gorgeous night.

RUTH: Not bad.

TONY: I had to come out here – got a bit hot. Done too much dancing. Thought I'd stay till sun-up. Watch the sun rise.

RUTH: Don't think the beer'll last.

TONY: Best time, see – first peek of orange and the day waiting to be created.

RUTH: Yeah.

TONY: So. Just to clarify. This is a no-snog situation, is it?

RUTH: One hundred per cent.

TONY: You're sure about that.

RUTH: One thousand per cent.

TONY: Final answer?

RUTH gives him an old-fashioned look.

Right. Does that also cover blow-jobs?

RUTH: I would have thought so.

TONY: Okay. Good. Just thought I'd check.

RUTH: Here with your mates?

TONY: If you can call them that.

RUTH: What d'you mean?

TONY: All they've talked about – all night, mind – is hi-fi components. Which one's got the best output, RMS, separates, magazine ratings – *all* night!

RUTH: Nice.

TONY: They're a sorry excuse for a bunch of friends.

RUTH: How long have you known them?

TONY: Eighteen years. Same schools then same pubs. Only the trousers have got longer. I might sack them.

RUTH: What?

TONY: I'd let them down gently. Sorry lads, I'm gonna have to let you go. I need a bit of new blood so I've put an ad in Tuesday's *Evening News*. Don't take it personal, but your one pound fifty aftershaves and obsessions with fuses really aren't doing any of us any favours. So…thanks for all the beer and, well, goodbye. (*He smiles.*) So what d'you do then?

RUTH: Me?

TONY: Yeah. You.

RUTH: I don't do anything.

TONY: You must do something.

RUTH: (*Tetchy.*) I don't. I do nothing. Make no contribution to society whatsoever. Next question.

TONY: Easy tiger.

RUTH: I work out at the airport.

TONY: Doing what?

RUTH: I cater.

TONY: For what?

RUTH: For the planes. I assemble airline meals. I cut up

lettuce and stick the pieces in square containers with clear lids. All day. I'm hoping for promotion. Then I get to put cherries in the centres of pineapples. It's fantastic.

TONY: D'you ever, like, you know, gob in them?

RUTH: Yeah. Quite a lot, actually.

TONY: Do you? Really?

RUTH: Yeah.

TONY: Ah, shit. I've ate them.

RUTH: I wouldn't if I were you.

TONY: What, like greenie gobs?

RUTH: (*Nodding.*) Chewier the better.

TONY: No!

RUTH: I can't afford to fly anywhere. Least I can do is gob on those who can.

TONY: I thought you'd get free flights and stuff.

RUTH: Oh yeah, they really want to keep us sweet, we're a right skilled workforce. Free flights! It's going on out there somewhere, mind. People getting free flights, jetting off on holiday. And there's me, catering for it. I feel like I haven't been paying attention. Like I got on the wrong train and now I'm not where I thought I was. I was supposed to be rich by now. Or famous. Or having loads of sex. Or all of that. Not none of it.

TONY: So if you could be anywhere now, where would you be? What would you do?

RUTH: Anywhere? At all?

TONY: At all.

RUTH: Bloody hell, you ask 'em.

TONY: Your dream place.

RUTH: I'd need a sec to think.

TONY: D'you want another?

RUTH: Yeah.

TONY goes up the steps to fetch them.

You coming back?

TONY: Left my lighter. (*He goes inside.*)

RUTH sits for a second. Then takes a lipstick and a tiny mirror out of her pocket. Applies the lippy.

EDIE'S VOICE: (*Football chant.*)
Get 'em off, get 'em off, get 'em off
Get 'em off, get 'em off, get 'em o-ff!

RUTH looks up. She freezes, holding the lipstick close to her mouth.

There is now a man's bottom in the window, again in flamboyant underwear.

He's dancing and preening.

RUTH: Oh my God…

DON'S VOICE: I hope you're ready for this, lady!

He parades a little more, accompanied by EDIE's cheering.

As he does so, TONY comes back out with beers. Sees RUTH and the arse. Delight.

TONY: See!!!

RUTH: That's not a woman's arse!

TONY: It's a different one!

RUTH: How can you tell?

DON'S VOICE: Here we go!

TONY: I can tell the difference between a man and a woman's arse!

RUTH: Well that's a relief.

DON'S VOICE: Back behind the velvet rope ladies!

EDIE'S VOICE: (*Triumphant conclusion to DON's strip.*) Wa-hey!

The figure disappears from the window.

RUTH: At least somebody's having fun.

TONY: We're having fun!

RUTH: Thanks for telling me.

TONY hands her a beer and sits.

TONY: Well?

RUTH: Oh. Yeah. Right. Greek island. One of them really tiny ones that no-one goes to. Like you see on the Holiday programme. Sunset. Little taverna on the beach. Big long empty stretch of shore. Little breeze. Clear water lapping gently away. Bottle of Amstel straight from the fridge, ice cold, frosted glass, outside of the bottle covered in that cold water sweat that happens. Cigarette. And nothing to do tomorrow. Or for ever.

TONY: (*Quietly.*) By yourself?

RUTH: Yeah.

TONY nods.

What about you?

TONY: Oh, don't ask me that.

RUTH: I told you.

TONY: Yeah.

RUTH: If you could be anywhere? Now.

TONY: You'll laugh.

RUTH: Anywhere in the world.

TONY: I'd be here.

RUTH: What, this shithole?

TONY: I wasn't talking about the place.

RUTH: (*Looking out.*) So warm tonight.

TONY: Yeah.

RUTH: I like this time. (*Looks at TONY.*) Tell me something then.

TONY: Eh?

RUTH: Anything.

TONY: Oh. Like what?

RUTH: I dunno. Something you wouldn't normally tell me now.

TONY: I had cancer.

RUTH: What?

TONY: You asked.

RUTH: When?

TONY: Two years ago.

RUTH: And you survived?

TONY: Miss Marple strikes again! How does she do it, Inspector?

RUTH: No. I mean, you're okay.

TONY: Touch wood.

RUTH: Bloody hell. What was it like?

TONY: Like I was looking in on someone else's life.

RUTH: What sort was it?

TONY: Oh. Well. It was a…real…man's cancer.

RUTH: How d'you mean?

TONY: Y'know.

RUTH: No.

TONY: You know…

RUTH: I don't know!

TONY: I dropped a bollock!

RUTH: (*Trying not to smile.*) Oh.

TONY: Walk lighter on the left these days.

RUTH can't help giggling.

TONY smiles and watches her.

She calms down.

RUTH: Sorry.

TONY: Well, you've blown it now.

RUTH: I couldn't help it.

TONY: They ask you if you want a replacement. But apparently it floats in the bath. I thought sod that for a game of soldiers.

RUTH: Has it made any difference to…?

TONY: No, I'm still a blinding fuck, don't worry.

RUTH: In your dreams.

TONY: And maybe in yours.

RUTH: Keep wishing, pal. Did it change your life?

TONY: No. Things don't work like that. Worst bit was telling my parents. Took 'em to the pub. Deserted Saturday afternoon. They knew something was up. Think they thought I was gonna tell 'em I was gay. They tried not to show. But it was in their eyes. Their small hours of the morning fear: 'Our son'll die before us.' Even now, my dad says, in that kind of all blokes together way, 'So you're *alright* are you?' Yes Dad. Thanks. My gran was the best. She said: does that mean he'll only be able to have boys, or girls? I meant to tell you, sex has started inside. Allegedly.

RUTH: Who?

TONY: Not sure. Bathroom's now officially out of service. Seven people missing. Money was on you and me for a couple of seconds 'till someone looked out the window and realised we were out here talking.

RUTH: (*Panic.*) Does Neil know we're talking?

TONY: Which one's Neil?

RUTH: Tall. Thin. Flowery orange shirt.

TONY: Not a rugby player then.

RUTH: No.

TONY: Quite pissed?

RUTH: (*Defensively.*) Perhaps.

TONY: I think he's playing Trivial Pursuit with my mates.

RUTH: That'll be him. Pub quiz on legs.

TONY: I looked in, but they all seemed on the verge of passing out.

RUTH: Beer and trivia – this'll be one of his Top Ten Nights.

TONY: Would it be a problem if he knew we're talking? We're *only* talking, after all.

RUTH: He gets jealous. He adores me.

TONY: But he's not the one.

RUTH: I didn't say that. (*Fiery.*) Why'd you think I was gonna say that?

TONY: I'm sorry.

RUTH: (*Angry.*) You don't know me! Don't think you know me!

TONY: I'm sorry, I'm sorry. I didn't mean it.

RUTH: I am *with* Neil! D'you understand? Is that too difficult a concept to get your head round?

TONY: Look, I said I'm sorry didn't I?

RUTH: He's my boyfriend! Alright? He's asked me to marry him!

TONY: Wow. Marriage. You do get on well. Have you given him an answer?

RUTH: Not yet.

TONY: When did he ask you?

RUTH: Last Saturday afternoon. City won away for first time all season.

TONY: And what did you say?

RUTH: Said I'd think about it.

TONY: Last of the great romantics, eh? And have you? Thought about it?

RUTH: Nothing but. Said I'd tell him at party tonight. He said, great we can announce it.

TONY: I see. All happening tonight. So. How did you meet?

RUTH: In a pub.

TONY: Right. Course.

RUTH: Neil likes pubs.

TONY: Good man.

RUTH: Reckons you can sort out all life's problems over a pint.

TONY: That's what Middle East peace process needs. Man like Neil.

RUTH: Gets it from his Dad. Get that man within sniffing distance of a barrel and some pork scratchings and it all comes pouring out. But most I've ever heard him say to Neil's mum is, 'Two sugars love.'

TONY: Perhaps they've said everything.

RUTH: I wouldn't want to ever get like that. I've got loads to say.

TONY: So I see.

RUTH: If you stop talking…you might as well stop living. I mean, you only know you're alive 'cos other people, like, confirm it to you. By talking. Back to you. Don't you think?

TONY: Um –

RUTH: So if you stop talking, people stop talking to you and then you sort of stop living. 'Cos it's the only sign people know you're there. And if people stop knowing you're there, how do *you* know you're there, I mean you'd start to think well is me being here just a figment of my imagination, do I actually exist at all, 'cos no bugger's talking to me and how do I know and who do I ask and if I do ask someone what if they don't reply – that'll really hit a nerve. I think that's why I'm uncomfortable around deaf people. I'm worried I don't exist.

TONY: So you were in a pub.

RUTH: Oh yeah…and this pissed guy came over to me. I could smell him before he arrived, like a vat of Kouros. And he says, 'Do you believe in love at first sight or shall I walk past again?' And I said I hadn't really formed an opinion one way or the other but if he tried anything on I'd have his eye on the end of a cocktail stick. And he said, 'Leave it out, I'm only doing this for a tenner.'

TONY: And that was Neil.

RUTH: No, that was Frank. Neil was the bloke who bet him.

TONY: And now you're happy ever after.

RUTH: I could have done a lot worse. I couldn't stand being alone. Sitting in. What if no-one would have me?

TONY: I'm sure someone would.

RUTH: Can we talk about something else?

TONY: Okay.

They sit there. Awkward.

Before I was ill, I never really did anything. Never took a chance or a risk. Never talked to a beautiful girl for fear of rejection. Never tried for jobs 'cos I knew I wouldn't get them.

RUTH: And having cancer changed all that?

TONY: No. I'm still a coward. Just now I beat myself up about it.

RUTH: You're alright, y'know.

TONY: Oh. Great.

They both smile. They have got quite close together.

Ruth…

RUTH: Yes…?

They look at each other. Their faces are not far apart.

TONY: I know…but…I wondered…it's just…I…

Faces even closer.

EDIE'S VOICE: (*Moaning.*) Oh! Oh! (*Escalating pleasure.*) Ohhhh!!

TONY and RUTH look up.

EDIE's head is hanging out of the window, lolling back, eyes closed. She is almost horizontal. She continues to moan.

EDIE: Oh! Yes! Oh! *Just* there! Mmmmmm!

She continues to moan, enjoying it more and more.

TONY and RUTH look at each other.

TONY: (*Not knowing what to say.*) I…well…um…

EDIE continues loudly. Joyously.

They look back up. Transfixed.

EDIE's hitting her peak.

EDIE: Oh yes, oh yes, oh yes – (*A thought strikes her.*) Begonias! Don! We haven't done – oh! – the – mmm – plants! (*Something takes her by surprise.*) Oh! Oh yes! (*She gives herself over to it.*) Go on, just a bit, oh…just a little bit more…more…oh…oh… Oh…oh…oh…(*Cries out.*) Take me to THE RIVER! (*She relaxes after the exclamation.*)

TONY and RUTH breathe out.

DON's head pops up. He has removed himself from where he was, between EDIE's legs.

He nods happily to himself.

EDIE and DON go back inside the room.

TONY and RUTH breathe out.

TONY: Fag?

RUTH: (*Instantly.*) Yeah.

　They light up and smoke.

TONY: Where were we?

RUTH: (*Looks at him.*) You were about to say something.

TONY: Was I? Oh. Right. Yeah. That's right. It's just –

There is a cheer from inside the house.

Bloody hell, what now?!

RUTH: What was that?

TONY: Don't these people realise it's the middle of the night?

RUTH: (*Getting up.*) Might just have a look at –

TONY: (*His face a picture of disappointment.*) – yeah –

RUTH: – what all the noise is about –

TONY: – right –

RUTH: – probably some bollocks –

TONY: – yeah probably. Some bollocks. Maybe Neil's won at Triv.

RUTH: Yeah. Maybe.

She goes inside.

TONY sits there for a moment, reflecting. Then he slaps himself slow and hard on the forehead. Repeats. And again.

DON and EDIE appear at the top of the steps. They are carrying a handful of plants each. They see TONY. They watch him slap his head about four or five times, faster and harder. Then he stops.

TONY: Dickhead.

DON: Evening.

TONY jumps.

DON and EDIE walk down the steps and head over to the flower bed.

TONY: Oh. Hi.

EDIE: (*To DON.*) About here, d'you reckon?

DON: Good as any, I reckon.

They put the plants down. EDIE brings out a small hand trowel and starts digging. DON watches.

EDIE: (*Pauses; looks up.*) Well go and ask him, then.

DON: Oh yeah. Right.

EDIE begins to transfer the plants from their pots to the soil. She sings to herself.

DON walks over to TONY. Breathes out. Nods at TONY. TONY nods back. DON looks out into the night. Sighs and shakes his head to himself.

Beautiful night.

TONY: Yeah.

DON sits down next to TONY.

TONY looks uneasy.

DON: Good party?

TONY: (*Evaluating in the light of RUTH's previous comments.*) No. Well, yeah. Actually. I mean, I think so. Perhaps. Could be.

DON: I'm glad we've got that sorted out. Having a bit of a party of our own.

TONY: Apparently. (*Checks himself.*) I mean, oh, really?

DON: Got any condoms?

TONY: Pardon?

DON: It's just we were wondering.

TONY: What?

DON: I'll be straight. You know what we want? Curry flavour. Curry flavour condoms. Got any?

TONY: Well –

DON: Oh, say you have. Never tried 'em. I've seen 'em advertised on machines in gents. Edie doesn't believe me. So I said I'd ask while she brought the plants down.

TONY: Um –

DON: You look the type who'd know. Are they more like korma or vindaloo?

TONY: Look, I don't –

DON: I'd pay you.

TONY: It's not –

DON: (*Bringing out a wad of cash.*) Hundred quid?

TONY: What?!

DON: Special occasion.

TONY: A hundred pounds if I can find you a curry flavour condom?

DON: Hoping to spice up our love life.

TONY: (*Energised.*) Stay there. I'll ask inside.

He gets up and runs up stairs in double quick time. He bumps into RUTH, coming out, who surveys the scene.

EDIE is still merrily gardening.

EDIE: (*Shouting across to DON.*) Has he got any?

RUTH: (*To TONY.*) What's going on out here?

DON: He's asking inside.

TONY: Don't worry. They're insane.

EDIE: Hey, love, come and give us a hand over here!

RUTH: (*To TONY.*) You're never going to believe this! There's a girl in there right, all the lads around her in a circle with her in the middle, tights round her ankles. Pissing to order, she is. Into a bucket. Stopping and starting when they shout. Someone says there's fifty pounds she couldn't do it five times. It's some sight.

TONY's smile freezes.

What's the matter?

TONY looks at RUTH.

TONY: That's my girlfriend.

RUTH: Your…?

TONY: Girlfriend. It's her party piece. She can earn more in a night than I do in a week.

RUTH: Your *girlfriend.*

TONY: Yes.

RUTH: And she's here?

TONY: And earning, by the sounds of it.

RUTH: You never said you…

TONY: I would've. It didn't really come up.

RUTH: How dare you.

TONY: I –

RUTH: How dare you!

TONY: Ruth, please –

RUTH: (*Getting to boiling point.*) You let me sit there and open up – and all along –

TONY: – just let me expl –

RUTH: – who are you anyway?! What am I doing talking to you? What am I thinking of? My boyfriend's inside!

TONY: Has he passed out yet?

RUTH: (*Defensive.*) No! Well, maybe! What's it got to do with you anyway? At least he's got two bollocks! I mean, who are you sitting out here with your one poxy testicle talking to me like we've known each other for years trying to make me think we've something in common? Eh? Thought you'd reel me in with some sob story like as if that's gonna work just cos I'm a bit drunk! I wouldn't touch you with a bargepole pal! This little chat of ours is well and truly over, now, d'you hear me, o-ver! Thank you and goodnight! Oh and you can shove your testicle up your arse!

EDIE and DON are staring at RUTH.

RUTH: (*Still on one; to DON and EDIE.*) And what the *hell* are you two doing?!

EDIE: Gardening.

RUTH: It's three in the morning! (*Taking a closer look.*) And anyway, you can't plant those outside! They'll die in a week!

EDIE: Will they? Oh no!

RUTH: Don't you know anything about plants?

EDIE: I've some more upstairs – will you come and take a look at them for me, tell me what to do?

TONY: Ruth…

RUTH: (*Turning her back on TONY; to EDIE.*) Yeah. Why not. Nice to know someone'll appreciate me.

EDIE and RUTH go into the house.

TONY exhales.

DON: She's a bit harsh, that one.

TONY: You noticed.

DON: (*Looking out into the night.*) Got a sewing machine?

TONY: Not on me.

DON: At home.

TONY: Er…no.

DON: No. No bugger has these days. I used to sell 'em. After the war. Made me money on Singers and the like. Nobody had any money to buy clothes, see. So they made their own. Machines made it all possible. I never had single unhappy customer. We had a Rolls, a boat, foreign cruises. I lived like a king on the back of them machines. What d'you do then?

TONY: I work in a call centre.

DON: Call centre?

TONY: For an accident claims company. They advertise on the telly.

DON: What the flamin' hell's a call centre?

TONY: There's two hundred of us. We take calls. Answer

queries. Pass information on to the claims specialists.

DON: You answer phones?

TONY: Well, yes, but –

DON: That's women's work! Telephonist! That's you, is it?

TONY: I suppose so.

DON: You're not that way inclined, are you?

TONY: What? Oh. No.

DON: Not that I've got anything against them. They're always in good shape. Look after themselves. More than can be said for lads like you.

TONY: Eh?

DON: You're not exactly fit, are you.

TONY: Oy!

DON: Take ten years off of me and I could have you on ground in thirty seconds. It's only age preventing me. You've no prowess, I can sense that. So what's your skills then?

TONY: Sorry?

DON: What skills d'you need to work in a call centre?

TONY: Well, you need to be polite…good with people… good phone voice…computer skills.

DON: Not much of a job, is it?

TONY: I don't think I'll be doing it for much longer. They're moving them to India. Cheaper.

DON: And what'll you do then?

TONY: I'll find something.

DON: You could do worse than be a salesman, you know.

TONY: I'm not sure I'd be right.

DON: Well, you'd need training obviously. I could give you a few pointers.

TONY: Really. It's fine.

DON: Suit yourself. If you don't want to learn. Got it bad then, have you?

TONY: Sorry?

DON: For the little 'un.

TONY: I only met her tonight.

DON: They spear you. Then you're buggered. Luscious lips.

TONY: I beg your pardon?

DON: Blow-job lips.

TONY: Who has?

DON: That lass of yours. Soon as I saw her, I thought, by 'eck, I bet she plays a good pink oboe.

TONY: D'you mind?!

DON: Oh, you're pinin' aren't you. Sorry. So you've fell for her, then?

TONY: She's got a boyfriend.

DON: Oh. That's that knackered.

TONY: And my girlfriend's inside.

DON: They always get narky about things like that.

TONY: Yeah.

DON: They're not natural sharers, women.

Both men nod.

TONY: I've been feeling sick for an hour now. I look at her

and my nerve endings do loops.

DON: Sounds like a bad case.

TONY: I've only just met her.

DON: Ah, you know. When it's love, you know.

TONY: Everyone says that. It really pisses me off. She's not gonna look at me. Her boyfriend's asked her to marry him. I wouldn't want to put her in an awkward position.

DON: (*Dirty grin.*) I flippin' would.

TONY: It wouldn't be fair. I wouldn't want to let her down. It's not worth the risk. Anyway, you heard what she said. I mean, I think she's amazing, but…it's a no-go. Not worth it.

DON: And that's that, is it?

TONY: Suppose it'll have to be.

DON: Pillock.

TONY: Eh?

DON: You lot, you think you can get everything if you've got a credit card and a remote control. Anything trickier than that and you start getting a bit panicked. So you miss your pivotal moments.

TONY: What?

DON: The *openings*. You spend your life selling, you can spot it in people's eyes. The shiny sparkling second. Hesitate and you miss it – sale's gone. Grab it and the world shifts. Imagine you're out somewhere, you catch a lady's eye. Smile, few glances. You get up courage and talk to her – nothing wrong with that, only conversation. But at some point, there'll be this interruption. A jump in the rhythm that's developed and *there*, right there at that point, she's thinking I wish he'd ask me something now because I might just say yes.

TONY: But what if –

DON: Hey! Shut up! I'm giving you gold here! That's the pivotal moment. The time to grasp life by the collar and say you're flamin' coming with me. And I bet I know what you do. With your shabby hair and your baggy trousers.

TONY: What?

DON: Absolutely nothing. And the moment slips through your fingers and goes crashing to the floor. Gone. Don't watch, lad. Participate.

The two women appear at the top of the steps, carrying a couple more plants.

Now do I have to go and find these chuffin' condoms meself?

TONY: Come with me.

DON: (*To EDIE.*) Is that the lot?

EDIE: All done. This young lady's going to help me bed 'em down.

TONY: (*To DON.*) Why are you doing this?

DON looks at EDIE. Sad smile.

DON: Come on, curry hunt.

EDIE and RUTH put the plants down and busy themselves.

DON and TONY go inside.

EDIE: Feeling a bit calmer, now?

RUTH: Yeah. Sorry. I've a bit of a temper. I don't drink much, see. And when I do…

EDIE: No apologies necessary. Well, not to me anyway.

RUTH: (*Helping EDIE.*) Why are we doing this?

EDIE: Don't you think they look nice down here?

RUTH: It's not that. It's just...why are you taking all the plants from your flat and replanting them outside, here?

EDIE: I only forget to water them. It's always Don has to remind me. Too lazy to do it himself, mind. Says green things bring him out in a rash. (*She drifts. For a moment she seems miles away.*). Got someone special, yourself?

RUTH: Neil.

EDIE: Oh dear, is that his name?

RUTH: What's wrong with Neil?

EDIE: I've never met an inspiring Neil. Is yours inspiring?

RUTH: He's duty manager at a car hire franchise.

EDIE: Oh. Is that good?

RUTH: We get free cars. You know, when they're not booked out. Mostly we get Clios, but we've had a Probe couple of times lately.

EDIE: Oh. Well.

RUTH: He's on fast track. He'll be a franchise manager within six months.

EDIE: So what does he have to do in this job?

RUTH: Oh he's quite important. Some people return 'em with only half a tank full, see. That's not on. He has to lock up three times a week.

EDIE: I'm sure that sounds very nice.

RUTH: We'll probably have kids. House. Some kind of nice vehicle.

EDIE: Nice?

RUTH: Yeah.

EDIE: Mmm.

Beat.

So what are you toying with this other one for?

RUTH: Who said I was toying?

EDIE: Hey, I've done enough toying in my time. I can spot it at ten yards.

RUTH: We just got to talking. He makes me laugh.

EDIE: Doesn't Neil?

RUTH: No. Not really. You know…to be honest… sometimes… Neil's a bit… Well, boring.

EDIE: (*Clapping her hands.*) I knew it! That's Neils all over!

RUTH: I can't believe I just said that! I didn't. I didn't say that. You didn't hear me say that! That's awful. Poor Neil.

EDIE: I bet he is though.

RUTH: Yeah. He is a bit. He loves hammering. I've never seen a bloke so much in love with an object. Anything that even vaguely needs knocking in or pulling out, Neil's like 'Oooh, I'll get me hammer'. He's got seven different ones. Says you can't have too many specialist tools.

EDIE: At least he knows how. Don can't put up his hand straight, let alone a set of shelves. He used to send men round from his workshop any time something practical needed doing. Useless, he is. But I don't know what I'd do without him. (*She catches herself. Stops.*) Am I doing this right?

RUTH: Like you were born to it.

EDIE: D'you know, I've been with that great lump all my life. I…

RUTH: Are you alright?

DON: (*Appearing at the door; brandishing a condom like the FA Cup.*) Currr-rreeee!!!

EDIE: (*Jerked back to reality.*) Don't tell me you found one!

TONY: That's the most expensive bunk-up you'll ever have.

DON: That's what you think!

EDIE: Donald!

DON: And you thought they didn't exist! Believe me now, do you?

EDIE: Well, daft inventions!

DON: Might as well make use of it, though.

EDIE: Oh well if you insist.

DON: (*To TONY.*) Do us a favour, lad. Finish off bedding them plants, will you? I'll bring you the cash down in a bit. Me and Edie have got a lot on the agenda.

TONY looks at RUTH.

RUTH looks down.

TONY: Okay.

DON: Come on Edie.

EDIE gets up. She looks at RUTH.

EDIE: Don't be scared.

DON: See you later, pal.

TONY: Don't wear yourself.

DON: Conked out on the job – what a way to go, eh?

TONY: Hey!

DON and EDIE continue up the steps.

TONY: Don!

DON: (*Turning.*) What?

TONY: If you made so much money…how come you're still living here?

DON: (*Smiles.*) You sound like my flaming wife.

They disappear back inside.

TONY and RUTH are left alone.

TONY: Hi.

RUTH: Hi.

TONY: (*Nodding to the plants.*) D'you know what you're doing?

RUTH: Should do. I've an allotment down Archers Road.

TONY: Really?

RUTH: (*Kneeling and setting to work.*) Girls all laugh at me. 'Off to her shed again!' they say. But I love it down there. Everything you put in, you get back ten times over.

TONY is just sitting looking at RUTH. She notices.

TONY: I just wan –

RUTH: (*simultaneously.*) I didn't m –

They both smile.

TONY: Don't you hate that?

RUTH: After you.

TONY: No, no…nothing…just… What were you going to…?

RUTH: Oh. I…I'm sorry. I didn't mean what I said.

TONY: About me sticking my testicle up my arse?

RUTH: Yeah. That.

TONY: Good. Because I'd hate to have to try it.

They continue to work.

RUTH: So, what were you two talking about?

TONY: Eh?

RUTH: You and the old feller?

TONY: Oh. You know…football…stuff.

RUTH: Right.

TONY: How about you two?

RUTH: Oh. You know…dolls, periods. Stuff.

TONY: Right.

RUTH: All done.

They step back. Admire their handiwork.

TONY: What now?

RUTH looks inside the house.

RUTH: (*Reluctantly.*) I'd better see if –

TONY: (*Deep breath.*) D'you wanna sit down?

RUTH: (*Looking inside house.*) Um…

TONY: For a minute. Please?

RUTH sits down.

TONY: I'm sorry I didn't say...you know. It just didn't seem relevant. Not to this moment.

RUTH: How long have you been seeing her?

TONY: Six months. She picked me up when I was drunk. She's a lovely girl but it's like going out with an air-raid siren. She can squeal at the exact pitch to set off fax machines. She's not for me. We both know it.

TONY takes a deep breath.

RUTH: Tony, I –

TONY: Listen... I need to... Um... Say... I mean... I know we only met earlier... And I nearly set you on fire... And we're both going out with people. Obviously that's quite tricky. But... Well... You are the most beautiful woman I have ever laid eyes on in my entire life. I saw you and my heart leapt. You make me want to change my life. To...participate. I know it's not possible and that you have a boyfriend and we're not...compatible or whatever but... I just... I know it's stupid... but maybe just hear me out for a second and then you can tell me I'm an idiot and we'll both go back in and pretend this never happened but... I want to travel the world with you. I want to bring the ice cold Amstel to your Greek shore. And sit in silence and sip with you. I want to go to Tesco's with you of a Sunday. Watch you sleep, scrub your back, rub your shoulders, suck your toes. I want to write crap poetry about you, lay my coat over puddles for you, always have a handkerchief available for you. I want to get drunk and bore my friends about you, I want them to phone up and moan about how little they see me because I'm spending so much time with you. I want to feel the tingle of our lips meeting, the lock of our eyes joining, the fizz of our fingertips touching. I want to touch your fat tummy and tell you you look gorgeous in maternity dresses, I want to stand

46

next to you wide-eyed and hold my nose as we open that first used nappy, I want to watch you grow old and love you more and more each day. I want to fall in love with you. I think I could. And I think it would be good. And I want you to say yes. You might feel the same.

Beat.

Could you? Maybe?

RUTH looks at TONY.

She goes to say something.

Snap blackout.

The chorus of 'Don't Falter' by Mint Royale crashes in, loud and joyous.

End of Act One.

ACT TWO

Twenty-ish minutes later.

We can no longer see the ground floor and garden. The house has moved down a level. The first floor now rests on the stage. It has opened out to reveal DON and EDIE's flat. Above it, we see the top and outside of the house leading up to the roof. A metal fire escape staircase lines the left side of the house.

The sun is beginning to rise, bathing the exterior in a beautiful glow which progresses along with the Act.

'Just One Look' by Doris Troy plays. After the first three lines of vocals, the lights come up.

EDIE and DON's flat. Filled with mementoes of two shared lives. Old, previously expensive carpet, now tatty. Ditto the furniture. End of Empire feel.

After a little of the song, EDIE dances in. Sings, beautifully, passionately along with the song. As she does this, she begins to gut the flat. She flings open all the cupboards and pulls out every single bottle that she can find. She places them all together on the large dining table. She's creating mess. Boisterous. There is a handwritten piece of A4 pinned randomly to the wall which is headed 'AGENDA'.

After another verse, DON comes in, also dancing and singing. The two of them dance a perfectly orchestrated routine, singing all the words. They continue to empty all the drink cupboards onto the table – lots of glasses, too.

The two characters are both full of life and physically agile. They retain the verve of eighteen year olds.

DON: Flamin' Nora, Edie, my old feller feels like it's done ten rounds with Henry Cooper!

EDIE: That smell's still haunting me. Curry and rubber, eurgh.

DON: Lucky I wasn't set on using it.

EDIE: (*Proud.*) I promised you a good 'un though, didn't I?

EDIE brings out a bottle of champagne from the back of the cupboard. It's very dusty. She places it at the front of the table.

DON: What're you doin'?!

EDIE: It's our bottle!

DON: What's it sitting there for?

EDIE: I thought – just before – we'd have it.

DON: It's our rainy day champagne.

EDIE: We'll have it with sunrise instead.

DON: But –

EDIE: (*Suddenly stern.*) No arguments, Don. We agreed.

DON: Alright.

EDIE: No point it just sitting there.

DON: That beef and kidney was terrific and all.

EDIE: Butchers on Smethwick's. He's allus had an eye for me. Right.

DON: How long have I got?

EDIE: About fifty minutes. Sun rises four fifty-two or thereabouts. That's what paper reckons anyway.

DON: Doesn't time fly when you're having fun. Are we starting these or what?

He picks up a bottle and unscrews the top. Picks a random glass and pours a bit in.

(*To himself.*) Doesn't time fly when you're having fun.

EDIE: Rule is nothing's to be left at end. Finish all bottles. No light sips.

DON pours the remnant of the bottle into his glass.

DON: Come on then, girl, you know I never drink alone.

EDIE obeys.

Down the hatch.

They chink glasses and neck their drinks. They slam glasses down and shiver and shake their heads simultaneously at the shock of the old booze.

EDIE: Ooooh.

DON: What was that?

EDIE: Something we brought back from Yugoslavia that time.

DON: No wonder they're allus fighting.

EDIE: Right, I've a quiz, then a questionnaire and then, well…anyway.

DON: You're the boss, boss.

EDIE: Can't put it off forever.

DON: No.

EDIE: (*Breezy.*) I've five questions. And prizes go up, like on Millionaire. First off, it's old drinks and they get better more questions you get right.

DON: Can we open champagne if I get last one?

EDIE: I've said, champagne's for just before.

DON: But –

EDIE: I've got it planned, Don. Stop trying to disrupt me.

DON: Tonight of all nights, I should be allowed me own way!

EDIE: Well, you're not. So shut up about it. Question One.

She surveys the drinks. Picks out a bottle.

They start off easy, get you into it. So. For the last of the Sambuca we got in Venice in 1961, what's so special about today?

DON: You mean –

EDIE: Apart from the obvious. What's today?

DON: Fifty year.

EDIE: Fifty year what?

DON: You know what.

EDIE: Oy, you, play game!

DON: You reckon we had our first kiss fifty year ago tonight.

EDIE: He remembers! Bling! He gets the Sambuca! Hooray!

DON: I wouldn't have known. And neither would you if you hadn't found that old diary.

EDIE: Shut up and drink.

DON downs it.

Oh, and you can have three of them lifelines and all.

DON: Come on then.

EDIE: Question two, can you remember first time we laid eyes on each other? For a beer.

DON: Flamin' 'eck. First time. Let me think. That's right. You were standing on the edge of that loch, waving a bright red hanky at me. I was out in the boat just having a moment to myself, rowing all gently. And I thought, who's that lunatic waving a pair of red knickers?

Beat.

EDIE: What are you talking about?

DON: Eh?

EDIE: That's not how we met.

DON: Isn't it?

EDIE: No.

DON: Oh. (*Quiet.*) Bollocks.

EDIE: He forfeits the beer – it's mine.

She opens it and drinks it.

(*Teasing DON.*) Ooh, lovely. Beer. Mmmm.

DON: I was looking forward to that.

EDIE: That'll teach you.

DON: (*Bewildered.*) Well, if it wasn't –

EDIE: We were at a dance.

DON: Oh! Aye! That's right. In The Mood. Course! Boat was later.

EDIE: I've never waved a red hanky at you. Come to think of it, I've never seen you row a boat.

DON: (*Panicking.*) Haven't you?

EDIE: Who'd you meet by a loch?

DON: Oh, I don't know. Probably dreamt it. Goin' bloody mental.

EDIE looks at him suspiciously. DON carries on regardless.

That dance, eh?

EDIE: Ooh, sometimes, Don…I don't know why I stuck with you.

DON: Big in the trouser department.

EDIE: Says you. Red hanky, indeed.

DON: Come on next one.

EDIE: For the...Ouzo.

DON: I didn't know we still had Ouzo!

EDIE: It's been in cupboard ten years!

DON: I wish I'd known! I'm partial to a bit of that.

EDIE: For the Ouzo...where d'you keep the remote control for the telly?

DON: (*Indignant.*) What d'you need to know that for?!?

EDIE: Twenty years and you've never let me have it!

DON: (*Stubborn.*) I'm not telling you.

EDIE: You're impossible!

DON: I know what you like to watch!

EDIE: That'll not be any use to me, will it? Come on, I'm gonna have to hurry you.

DON struggles with his conscience.

DON: (*Grudgingly.*) It's behind the encyclopedia.

EDIE reaches behind her to check. Finds it. Brandishes it like a gladiator.

EDIE: Bling! You can have the Ouzo then.

DON: Oh, lovely.

He sips merrily.

EDIE: (*In full quizmistress mode.*) Now. You're half cut. Nobody can take that away from you. But we want to make sure you're completely hammered. D'you want to carry on?

DON: (*Grinning.*) Get on with it, you daft old trout. I've somewhere to be!

EDIE: For the single malt –

DON: – I love that malt –

EDIE: Where did we go on our fifth wedding anniversary?

DON: This is for the malt, is it?

EDIE: It is.

DON: And if I get it wrong, you'll drink it?

EDIE: I will.

DON: Fifth wedding anniversary.

EDIE: D'you want to phone a friend?

DON: Aye, go on then. I'll phone Fred.

EDIE: (*Picking up the phone and dialling.*) And where's Fred?

DON: He's five doors down. You know he is.

EDIE: Fred, it's Edie! Alright, love, yes, sorry to wake you. No, we don't sleep much these days either. Now listen, the next voice you'll hear will be Don's. No, we're quizzing it for fun. Yes. He's playing for the single malt. I will, love.

DON: (*Taking phone.*) Fred, where did me and Edie go for our fifth anniversary? (*Fred speaks.*) Oh yeah. That's right. Thanks Fred, mate. Yeah. (*He hesitates as if wanting to say something.*) Fred, I just wanted to say –

EDIE: (*Lightning quick.*) Say goodbye, Don!

DON: Goodbye Fred. (*He puts the phone down.*) I just wanted to say –

EDIE: You know the rules. We've to stick to them.

DON: I know, love. I'm sorry. It's like there's this big dark-

EDIE: (*Refusing to let him talk.*) For the single malt, where did we go for out fifth anniversary?

DON: (*Reluctantly.*) You took me to see the shop you'd spotted for me to buy. (*Buying into the memory slowly.*) We sat on the steps and drank Perry and talked about what we'd do. (*Smiling.*) And I told you in ten years we'd be millionaires.

They both smile.

EDIE: You weren't far wrong, as it turned out.

DON: People round here still remember. I've been in Coral's and they've said, whatever happened to the Roller you used to have?

EDIE pours the last of the whisky into DON's glass.

EDIE: Single malt.

DON: (*Taking in the aroma, sniffing the glass.*) God's own drink.

EDIE: Question five.

DON: Make it an easy one. I'm feeling bit wobbly now.

EDIE: It'll be good anaesthetic. For the vintage port.

DON: Not the champagne?

EDIE: Not yet!

DON: We've had that champagne forty eight years now – you've always found some excuse not to open it and tonight's just the same.

EDIE: Maybe I will, maybe I won't. For the port... How much do you love me?

DON: Will you just ask question five!

EDIE: That is question five.

DON: Oh. (*Serious.*) With every ounce of my being, for ever and ever amen.

EDIE: Bling! He's won the vintage port.

DON: Oh yes! You'll have to help me out.

EDIE: I'll have a little.

She pours DON a huge glass and herself a medium sized one.

DON drinks.

Down down down! Quicker lad!

DON can't neck it all at once.

DON: (*Gasping for breath.*) I can't!

EDIE: (*Laughing.*) Come on, you seven stone weakling. We've all this to get through. (*Tips the glass back to his mouth and forces him to drink again.*) Deal's a deal. Nothing's happening unless you drink!

DON: (*Pushing her hand away and laughing.*) Flamin' eck, woman are you trying to kill me?

He and EDIE laugh. They start laughing at his joke and then the laughter gets stronger and stronger until they are both roaring with fantastic, infectious laughter. DON is slapping his leg in amusement, EDIE is hooting and wiping away tears of laughter. They laugh and laugh and laugh for an incredibly long time and just as you think it's subsiding, they start laughing all over again, as if at some fresh new joke. It maybe lasts two or three minutes.

The laughter than gradually dies down. They've really enjoyed it. It fades down gradually into giggles, then smiles, then quiet. Then total silence as realisation hits them.

The silence that follows is ice cold. DON and EDIE just sit there. Silence. A real long ache of silence. After a while. DON winces with pain.

Best take me pills.

He picks up a bottle of industrial strength painkillers and shakes a couple out.

EDIE watches him, worried.

EDIE: Have you had a nice day?

DON: It's been…everything.

EDIE: I was worried. That you wouldn't enjoy it.

DON: I've been with you. It's enough. You've to be careful about fingerprints. You know that don't you?

EDIE: Don!

DON: And you've got enough of the stuff?

EDIE: Yes! Now, will you stop going on! Time's getting on. I want to do the questionnaire.

DON: What is this questionnaire, anyway?

EDIE: Like they have in the *You* magazine.

DON: D'you think we should ring the lad again?

EDIE: It's middle of day in Australia, now. He'll be at work.

DON: I worry what he'll think.

EDIE: *(Firmly.)* I need you to be strong.

DON: I'm worried the letter isn't enough.

EDIE: He's his own life, now. We did as best we could for him.

DON: I never thought he'd make a go of it out there.

Never thought he was strong enough. But look at him now. Doing better than I was at his age. Will he forgive me?

EDIE: Please Don.

DON: There seems so much to think of. Like packing for holiday. Worried you've forgotten something.

EDIE: We've been thorough enough.

DON: Did you get me some cigarettes? Like I asked?

EDIE: On the side.

DON gets up. Goes over to the side. Picks up a pack of Woodbines.

DON: (*Amazed.*) Woodies! Where did you get these?

EDIE: They were your favourite, weren't they?

DON: You're the best woman ever lived.

He turns his back on EDIE and sets to lighting a cigarette.

EDIE: Right, you have to answer these quick as possible, not really thinking. Number one. What's your current state of mind.

DON: Bloody blissful.

He turns round. He has five Woodbines in his mouth and is puffing madly away on them.

EDIE: What are you doing?

DON: Thought I'd make the most of it. I'm invincible, me.

EDIE: Tell us a secret.

DON: (*Mouthful of ciggies.*) Eh?

EDIE: Number two: tell us a secret.

DON: What like?

EDIE: I don't know. Something about me – that you've never told me before.

DON: Um...

DON thinks about it for a moment. He takes a joyous, five ciggie puff.

EDIE: There must be something. Have a think.

DON: You'll not like it.

EDIE: Eh?

DON: If I tell you what I'm thinking, you'll get the hump.

EDIE: We've no secrets!

DON: Well, there is this one.

EDIE: You'd better tell me then, mister.

DON: I wish I hadn't started this, now.

EDIE: Come on, spit it out!

DON: I've never liked your way with eggs!

EDIE is gobsmacked.

EDIE: I beg your pardon?

DON: I told you you'd get the hump!

EDIE: What d'you mean, my way with eggs?

DON: Just that.

EDIE: I've all different ways with eggs!

DON: And all of 'em terrible.

EDIE: What – scrambled, poached –

DON: What's next on that questionnaire of yours?

EDIE: (*Unstoppable.*) – fried, boiled –

DON: All of them.

EDIE: So you're saying all those eggs I've ever done for you –

DON: I could never work out what it was. But you and eggs should have had one of them exclusion zones around you, like the Falklands.

EDIE: Even egg and chips?!?

DON: They just never came out right. Words I most dreaded hearing: 'I've got some nice eggs in for your tea.'

EDIE: Why didn't you ever say anything?!

DON: It's not my place, is it? A man telling a woman how to do things in kitchen.

EDIE: Is that why Barry used to call me Cool Hand Luke?

DON: I might have mentioned something to him down pub.

EDIE: Well, I tell you. You think you know someone. Eggs. Eggs! And he never said anything.

DON: Look, the sky's beginning to lighten. I'll be off in half an hour, woman. We haven't got time to quarrel about eggs. Not as last thing.

EDIE: Hmph.

DON: Ask me another.

EDIE: (*Reading.*) When and where were you happiest?

DON: Wigan Casino. All those Saturday nights.

EDIE: Really?

DON: We were oldest ones there and I loved it.

EDIE: I never thought you were that bothered about music. Just thought you suffered it for me 'cos I liked going.

DON: Some of those songs. They make me skin tingle. That one we had earlier. Just One Look.

EDIE: Doris Troy.

DON: I always loved that. On towards the end of the night. Classic. That were always our song, for me. (*A thought strikes him.*) When it…you know…when you're… Will you sing to me? Sing that song to me. Just One Look. That'd be the way. (*He smiles.*) Is that all of them?

EDIE: Eh?

DON: The *You* magazine thingies.

EDIE: Oh. I've got one. It's not quite from the paper.

DON: Go on.

EDIE: I was wondering…

DON: Yeah.

EDIE: The money.

DON: What about it?

EDIE: Where did it all go?

Beat.

DON: I wondered if you'd ever ask me. You never said anything at time. But some nights, I could see question on your face.

EDIE: I trusted you with it all. More fool me, eh?

DON: Maybe.

EDIE: Tell me what happened. I'd always thought we were well off.

DON: We *were*. We had over thirty great years off those machines. I worked night and day for those shops.

EDIE: We hardly saw you.

DON: Because I was workin' all the hours.

EDIE: Not all the time. Not at two am.

DON: Deliveries.

EDIE: Aye. Delivering money to card-tables.

DON: I don't know why you've always thought that.

EDIE: Because I'd be in butcher's and some woman'd say, 'Your old man had the shirt off my Jack's back last night and I hope it chokes him.'

DON: I had a little game now and again, that's all. People just stopped buying. It was a mystery. What it is to go out of fashion. What's gonna be more appealing to a young lass than sitting at a good machine, foot poised above the pedal, making herself a nice new dress. Or doing her fella's turn-ups. What could be more exciting than that? Market slowed up. I thought it'd be up and running again within a couple of months. When it wasn't, I tried the tables. Speculate to accumulate.

EDIE: Why didn't you tell me?

DON: What could you have done about it?

EDIE: I could have gone out to work. Given us a bit more money.

DON: What's the point in getting married if your husband can't look after you? All I wanted was the best for us. And we had it. I was on a winning streak too. The tables loved me. For a while. Giving it up, once you'd tasted it…it was harder than never having had it in the first place. I hated having to sell all those things.

EDIE: If only you'd bought this place when they offered.

DON: Didn't seem any point then. Waiting to buy a bigger one.

EDIE: And here we are still waiting. Still renting.

There is a banging at the door.

DON: Who the flippin' eck's that?

He goes to answer it. TONY bursts in, full of energy.

TONY: Sorry, sorry! You're still up are you?

DON: We are now.

TONY: It's just, that guy we got the condom off –

DON: What about him?

TONY: He's pestering me for the money.

DON: Oh aye! Course! I were going to bring it down. Sorry lad, got waylaid. So to speak.

He fetches his wallet from the side. TONY explains to EDIE.

TONY: I wouldn't have come up only I'm trying to…you know…talk to Ruth…and he keeps on interrupting. He's driving me mad.

EDIE: How's it going?

TONY: Well, that was the other thing I wanted to ask. (*To DON.*) You haven't got any more tips, have you? I mean, I did what you said, you know, took the moment, and it's going alright but…no sale, as yet.

DON: Flamin' Nora, lad, d'you want me to come down there and do it for you?

TONY: I just need one last bit of help.

DON considers for a second.

DON: I know just the thing.

TONY: Fantastic.

DON goes over to the table and picks up a bottle. Hands it to TONY.

What's this?

DON: Yugoslavian speciality.

TONY: But –

DON: Drastic times call for drastic measures.

TONY: I was thinking more about advice on what to say.

DON: Get enough of that down her, it won't make a blind bit of difference what you say.

TONY: Oh. Right. Good point. We have had a bit of a drink shortage, actually.

DON: That'll sort you out, you mark my words.

TONY: Thanks.

He goes to leave. Turns.

She is amazing. I've never, you know... (*Catches himself.*) Sorry. Bit over-excited. I'll...

He gestures that he's about to go. And goes.

DON looks at EDIE. It is as if the wind has been pulled out of him.

DON: (*Quiet.*) It's not fair.

EDIE: Don't.

DON: This...thing. It's not bastard fair.

EDIE: I can't keep strong if you –

DON: (*Crumbling.*) Why has this happened? Eh? Is it punishment? Is it him upstairs trying to even things out for all that good we had? Eh? Eh?

EDIE: We said we wouldn't. Our rules. Tonight is only the good things.

DON: I can't help it, Edie! I don't understand why –

EDIE: (*Trying to ignore it.*) No tears. No bad memories.
No darkness.

DON: Easy for you to say, lady! Bastard bloody easy!

EDIE: (*Beginning to crack.*) Oh it is, is it?

DON: It's not you giving up your breath is it? Not you
walking into the nothingness like some blinded old goat.

EDIE: Please, Don.

DON: I don't want to do it, Edie. I've changed my mind.
I forbid you.

EDIE: Please, don't.

DON: I forbid you, d'you hear me? Don't you come to me
with that needle. I'm not going anywhere, I'm staying
here with you. I'm not having you doing without me,
Edie, you're not coming near me with that needle, you
can sod off right back to where you came from and
that's an end to it, you are not going to you are not going to you are not going to bloody you are bloody not
going bloody to bloody bloody –

EDIE: (*Over him.*) *You listen to me, Donald Fielding!* I am
going to bloody kill you whether you like it or not! It's
what we agreed we've talked it through and out and over
and we're not diverting now alright? I'm not watching
you waste away. I'm not nagging you to take a dozen
daily pills, brushing clumps of your hair off pillow and
seeing skin hang off you like some too-big coat. You
promised, you said, 'I'm too full of life', and you are.
We end it. We put the full stop not some clumsy little
cancer. So just shut up and *fucking enjoy yourself* or I'll do
it right here and now and then who'll be sorry, eh?!

Beat.

DON: I've not heard you say the f word before.

EDIE: That's because I never have.

DON: Oh. I see.

EDIE: I'm a lady. Ladies don't say that sort of thing.

DON: Didn't know you knew those sorts of words.

EDIE: I know more words than you think. I'd not be at a loss for words without you.

DON: My father always said a man needs to know how to swear. Well timed swear word'll get you much further than a nice smile.

EDIE: I've heard them all in my time.

DON: Where have you heard words like that?

EDIE: I've been down the High Street. I've read magazines and books. I've seen television.

DON: Tell me some swear words, then.

EDIE: Don't be daft.

DON: No, come on.

EDIE: What, you want to me talk dirty to you?

DON: If you like.

EDIE: You old pervert.

DON: I'm allowed a treat, aren't I?

EDIE: Alright. (*Beat.*) Don't think I can't. Because I can.

DON: Come on then. Let's hear you.

EDIE: No rushing me!

DON: Get on with it!

EDIE: Right.

DON: Right.

EDIE: Here I go then.

DON: I'm all ears.

EDIE: Ass cheeks.

She looks to DON for approval. He nods.

That was on Channel Five. Late night erotic review. You were asleep.

DON: Is that it?

EDIE: Spunky. (*Another.*) Juicy spunky cum juice.

DON: By 'eck.

EDIE: Juicy spunky cum juice on my ass cheeks. What d'you think of that?

DON: I'm not rightly sure.

EDIE: (*Tipsily getting into her stride.*) And wank. I know wank. Wank your spunky cum juice on my ass cheeks. (*She's enjoying this.*) See, I know more than you think.

DON: I reckon that's about all, though.

EDIE: No. Fuck. Wank. Ass cheeks. Bollocks. Cunt. Cunt! Old lady saying cunt, that'd stop 'em down Horse and Jockey, I could go in and say gin and bitter lemon and fuckwank my arse cheeks with your bollocks you cunt and while you're about it shove that pulsing veiny big cock in my mouth shag bonk screw hump you and your purple buggery helmet you fuckfest all gism'd cunnilingus arse fisty fellatio blow job suck off like there's no tomorrow you great big licking sexy tit felcher.

She comes to a halt and breathes out. She's delighted with herself.

DON is staring open-mouthed at EDIE.

Oh. (*Remembering one other.*) Frottage.

She nods, satisfied. She's finished.

DON starts to laugh.

What's so funny?

DON: I knew I shouldn't let you watch late night telly.

EDIE: You thought you'd heard all my words, didn't you?

DON: Thank God we never got Sky, you'd've been arrested in street.

EDIE: You think you know everything, but I've got depths. I can swear. Now it's your turn.

DON: Me?

EDIE: Come on, Mr Big Man.

DON: I reckon you've got 'em all covered, love.

EDIE: Who d'you fantasise about?

DON: Eh?

EDIE: On the sly. Tell me. Any ladies who stir you?

DON: What's got into you?

EDIE: You, earlier on, you dirty tyke.

DON: Bloody hell, it's like I've opened floodgates and being caught in the deluge.

EDIE: In this magazine in the doctor's, they were saying it's healthy to have fantasy figures. And I thought I wonder who Don's is.

DON: Those magazines make a mint out of your like.

EDIE: You must have someone.

DON: I might have.

EDIE: Someone off the telly?

DON: Well...

EDIE: You used to like Hannah Gordon.

DON: I'm off her now.

EDIE: Who is it?

DON: That Charlie Dimmock. The one with the T-shirts.

EDIE: I knew it! I knew you had a thing for her. Haven't I said, when that comes on, haven't I said, 'What are you watching a garden programme for?' You go sneezy if there's pot pourri in the house, never mind gardens.

DON: I like a practical woman.

EDIE: D'you want to know who I like?

DON: No.

EDIE: Shall I tell you?

DON: No!

EDIE: Michael Portillo.

DON: WHAT?!?!

EDIE: He's very dashing.

DON: Portillo!?

EDIE: It must be his Spanish blood. Those lovely lips.

DON: It's grounds for divorce, this. The shame of it! Portillo!

EDIE: (*Defensive.*) He's always beautifully turned out.

DON: You don't stand a chance, anyway, he's an uphill gardener.

EDIE: That's all in his past. Youthful indiscretion.

DON: (*Shaking his head.*) Michael bloody Portillo.

EDIE: We've always had a laugh, haven't we?

DON: Oh aye.

EDIE: We have a joke.

DON: Aye.

EDIE: Don. I've something to tell you.

DON: Look, if you're worried about money –

EDIE: It's not that.

DON: It's all taken care of. I know there's not as much as there should be, but you'll be taken care of.

EDIE: Don, will you listen to me.

DON: What?

EDIE: I'm not gonna stay here.

DON: Eh?

EDIE: I'm not stopping here on me own.

DON: Oh. Well. That's your right, int it? Fred says sheltered accommodation's a godsend, you get your own warden and panic button –

EDIE: I'm coming with you.

Beat.

I'm not staying here. I'm coming with you. I've got enough insulin from my diabetes. I'll do you, then I'll do meself. I won't have to worry about leaving fingerprints on syringe then.

DON: Oh no. Oh no you don't, lady. I'm not having that.

EDIE: You've no choice.

DON: I've provided for you. I've done the will.

EDIE: I'm sure. But I don't want it. I want to be with you.

DON: No. No no no no.

EDIE: I don't want to be alone, Don.

DON: Edie, it's not right. I can't take you away from this. *I'm* ill. Not you.

EDIE: You'll not be taking. I've made a choice. *I've* got a choice.

DON: No.

EDIE: Don –

DON: I can't…think of you not living. Even after I'm…it's not right. It's not right.

EDIE: Listen to me, Don.

DON: I forbid you!

EDIE: You'll be in no place to do any forbidding, mister.

DON: I'll make meself known! I'll find a way. I'll haunt you! I'll come straight back as a poltergeist and scare the shite out of you.

EDIE: Please, just listen a moment. I've not slept these last three nights. Thinking. What I might do, how I might go on, without you. I tried to picture a day, but I couldn't even get past breakfast without cracking. I'd have to use bathroom first. I don't want to use bathroom first. I'll have to buy smaller toast loaves or they'll be stale by end of second day. I'll end up chatting to echoes. And all I'll see and hear and touch'll be space where you should be. And then, when I was down there tonight, talking to that girl, I realised. At sunrise, we go together. It's decided.

DON: But we don't know what's on the –

EDIE: I know. It's only a possibility but possibility is better than no chance. To do this gives me hope.

DON: But –

EDIE: I've gone along with you. Do the same for me.

DON: I see. I've seen that look before.

EDIE: My 'I shall not be moved' look.

DON: Bloody hell. You're a sod, Edie.

EDIE goes over to a bureau and brings out some papers.

EDIE: We'll need to change will. For Darren.

DON: Edie, are you –

EDIE: *No arguments!* We've better things to do with time we've got left.

DON: I can hand-write amendments. Give 'em here.

She does. Don sets to work. After a second, he stops.

What'll he say? With us both gone.

EDIE: He's been halfway across the world these seventeen years. We'll be as much with him as we are now. He'll understand. Eventually. He'll have to.

DON: We haven't got any witnesses. We need witnesses to the changes.

EDIE goes over to the window. Opens it and leans down, shouting.

EDIE: Hey, you two! You're wanted. Just get up here!

She closes the window and goes over to the hi-fi.

Put some music on for the young 'uns.

The intro to 'Que Sera' by The High Keys – a joyous Latino version – begins to play.

It's one of ours. Wigan Casino. Remember?

DON, unable to reply, just nods. EDIE grabs his hand. They dance perfectly, sometimes singing along to the upbeat, life-affirming dance hall track. The complex choreography they perform is obviously etched in their minds from their dance hall days. They dance as if their lives depend on it, wringing every ounce from every move, dancing together as one. It's essential and urgent.

Midway through the song, DON stops dancing. He stands there, hardly listening to the music, frozen with fear of what's coming, staring into the middle distance. Cold overtakes him. After a few moments, EDIE drags him gently back to reality and the dancing. They finish the song on a high.

Towards the end of the song, RUTH and TONY stand in the doorway watching. The song ends.

DON and EDIE collapse into chairs.

RUTH: Are we interrupting?

EDIE: Not at all. You're just what we need. Fresh faces.

RUTH: What *are* you two up to?

DON: Many things, love. The party to end all parties.

EDIE: Would you like a drink?

RUTH: What have you got?

TONY: What haven't they got, more like.

RUTH: (*Going over to the window.*) Wow, what a view. (*To TONY.*) The sky's just starting to get light.

DON and EDIE look at each other.

TONY: It's beautiful.

EDIE: (*Doing the drinks.*) I'll just take whatever comes to hand.

RUTH: So what was it you wanted?

DON: Oh. Yes. Well. How d'you fancy being witnesses?

TONY: Why, is there gonna be a crime?

EDIE: We'd like you to sign something.

RUTH: What?

DON: (*Producing papers.*) My will.

RUTH: Your will?!

DON: (*Breezily.*) I've just rejigged it and I need a couple of witnesses. (*To TONY.*) You *can* write, can't you?

TONY: Watch it, you.

RUTH: D'you make a habit of doing this stuff at four a.m.?

DON: We're nocturnal. We like to do everything this time of night.

TONY: So we saw. (*He takes a look at the will.*) So where d'you want us to sign?

DON: Just there.

He hands over a pen.

TONY signs. He hands the pen to RUTH.

RUTH: Can tonight get any stranger? (*She signs.*)

DON: Thanks very much.

EDIE: Cheers.

They all clink glasses.

RUTH flicks through the will absently while the following conversation takes place.

DON: (*To RUTH.*) So, you're thinking of taking him on

then?

TONY: Oy!

RUTH: What makes you think that?

DON: Well, he's mad keen on you.

TONY: D'you mind?!

DON: Not really.

TONY: We're at a delicate stage in negotiations. I bet it was easier when you were my age.

DON: Don't you believe it, son.

EDIE: (*Handing out drinks to TONY and RUTH.*) I had three boyfriends on the go when I met Don.

RUTH: (*Delighted.*) No!

EDIE: You have to keep your options open.

DON: You never told me that!

EDIE: Why would I want to tell you?

DON: You little minx.

EDIE: I wasn't going to ditch them and find out you were boring. You should be proud. You were the one I kept.

DON: (*To TONY.*) Don't ever kid yourself you've got the upper hand, son. Even now, she surprises me.

EDIE: (*To TONY.*) So d'you think you could love her, then?

RUTH: Hey!

TONY looks at RUTH.

TONY: Yeah. I'm certain.

EDIE: (*To RUTH.*) There you go. Not many'd say that straight off bat. To strangers and all.

DON: I don't suppose you two fancy a game of strip poker?

EDIE: Don!

DON: What?! A man can dream, can't he?

RUTH: (*Her attention caught by something in the will.*) Hang on a second. (*She looks up at DON.*) What's going on?

DON and EDIE exchange glances.

DON: What d'you mean?

RUTH: (*To EDIE.*) D'you know what he's done here?

EDIE: Erm…

TONY: What are you talking about?

RUTH: (*To EDIE.*) He's cut you out of the will!

DON: Look, lass –

RUTH: (*Outraged.*) He's left it all to someone called Darren and you won't see a penny! That's what he's changed! (*To DON.*) What are you playing at?

EDIE: Oh, look, I don't mind.

RUTH: Don't mind?!?! Are you mad?

EDIE: No, really. It's fine.

TONY: I'm not sure, you know. It does seem a bit out of order.

DON: What's it got to do with you?

RUTH: Hey! We're witnesses, remember! I wouldn't have signed if I'd known this was going on! I want my signature removing! I'll contest it! I'll –

DON: (*To EDIE.*) Shall we tell them?

RUTH is silenced for a second.

RUTH: Tell us what?

EDIE: You'll not stop us.

TONY: What's going on?

EDIE looks at DON.

DON: I've a tumour. Smack bang on the brain stem. In-operable. And spreading like wildfire. She's helping me go. Tonight. That's what we're celebrating.

EDIE: And after him, it'll be my turn.

DON: Late addition to the agenda. She'll not be argued with. Neither of us will. So don't bother trying. If you want to leave, we'll understand. Just don't try taking high ground.

EDIE and DON stare defiantly at RUTH and TONY.

TONY breathes out.

RUTH: I suddenly feel very sober.

EDIE: (*Pouring her another drink.*) No, that's not allowed.

RUTH: You're not serious about this.

DON: Deadly serious. And we don't need anyone judging us.

RUTH: (*To EDIE.*) You can't.

DON: (*To TONY; buoyant.*) How are you off for clothes?

TONY: Eh?

DON: I've some terrific things in there, come and see what you fancy.

TONY: What? I don't –

DON: They'll be no use to me, will they? Come on lad, I'm not offering twice.

He drags TONY out of the room.

EDIE and RUTH watch them go. Slight awkwardness.

EDIE: We weren't planning on telling you.

RUTH: Neil says I'm too nosey for my own good.

EDIE: Don says same to me! Cheeky sod.

Beat.

I wouldn't expect you to understand. Don calls it 'the least worst option'.

RUTH: For him, maybe.

EDIE: Fifty year we've been together. World's turned inside out in that time. He's the only thing I'm still certain of.

RUTH: You could live. Have a new life.

EDIE: But it wouldn't be any better.

Beat.

I can still see him that first night. He had a lovely suit. He talked rubbish at me all evening and when he smiled, I saw something in him.

RUTH: And that's when you knew?

EDIE: Course not. You never know right away. You don't sit at the side of a dance and think ooh, I bet he'll look good with dentures.

Beat.

There's nothing shameful about not wanting to live without him. That's what made it so beautiful all along.

DON re-enters. He is carrying a whole wardrobe's worth of clothes. We can barely see him beneath them. He throws them down on the sofa.

Behind him, TONY is equally laden, protesting.

TONY: But, Don –

DON: No, don't thank me! You can have 'em all!

TONY: I don't really –

DON: It's not rubbish, if that's what you're thinking.

TONY: It's not that.

DON: I were known for me dress sense. Had to be, in my line.

TONY: Don't take it the wrong way –

DON: There's a lovely blazer in there, be just your size.

TONY: Thanks. But really I couldn't.

DON: You don't want it?

TONY: Not really.

DON: (*To EDIE.*) He doesn't want it!

EDIE: Oh.

TONY: It's nothing personal.

DON: You should take a look at yourself, pal.

TONY: Give it to a charity shop.

EDIE: Guide Dogs for the Blind.

DON: I'm not giving it to some a load of flamin' dogs, I don't care how clever they are.

EDIE: Now you're just being awkward.

RUTH: Um, we should…leave you…to it. (*To TONY.*) You said you wanted to see the sun come up.

DON: (*To EDIE.*) Remember when we used to do that? (*To RUTH.*) We'd sneak up onto roof round about this time and watch it rise. Best view's up there.

RUTH: Thanks for the tip.

EDIE: Hang on, before you go. I've something for you.

She goes over to the table. Picks up the champagne. Hands it to RUTH.

DON: I don't bloody believe it!

EDIE: A little something to remember us by.

DON: Nigh on fifty year I've been waiting for that! And now she gives it away!

TONY: Are you sure?

EDIE: Course.

RUTH: It's really expensive.

EDIE: No. It's priceless. So use it well.

TONY: Thank you.

RUTH turns to DON.

RUTH: Do you believe in God?

DON: We'll tell you in an hour.

RUTH smiles. She and TONY go to leave. DON calls to them as they get to the door.

Hey!

TONY and RUTH turn.

Make sure those plants bloom alright.

TONY and RUTH leave.

Is it time?

EDIE: Very nearly.

DON: One last thing, then.

He goes over to the cupboard and starts rummaging.

EDIE: What are you doing?

DON: Aha!

He pulls out an old lipstick of EDIE's. Begins to scrawl on the mirror.

For those who find us.

He scrawls DON ♥ EDIE. Stands back. Admires it.

EDIE: Tasteful.

She pulls the equipment out of a drawer. Stands there for a second.

DON: (*Nervous.*) Got everything?

EDIE: Needles. Insulin.

DON: Will I go to hell? Will I see the Devil? Face to face and beg forgiveness? I've not been perfect, Edie. They'll know that. Will I be redeemed? Will I be redeemed?

EDIE: I'll redeem you.

DON: You?

EDIE: We've mitigation.

DON: What?

EDIE: Ourselves.

DON: I don't –

EDIE: We loved. Each other.

DON: Who'll sing to you?

EDIE: Pardon?

DON: If you're going to sing to me, who'll sing to you?

EDIE: I'll put Jimmy Radcliffe on.

DON: Yeah. Course. Last song of the night. Wigan Casino. You put Jimmy Radcliffe on.

EDIE: He can sing me away.

DON smiles at her.

DON: Good. It'd've bothered me. Is it time?

EDIE looks out the window.

EDIE: Yes.

DON: Oh.

EDIE: Are you ready?

DON: No.

EDIE: Me neither.

DON: Shall we do it then?

EDIE: Yes. Right then.

DON: Right then.

EDIE: This is it.

DON: This is it. So you'll be along in a minute.

EDIE: Yes. I'll be along.

She walks towards him.

DON: Can I say something?

EDIE: Please don't make it difficult.

DON: It's not that. I'm resolved. Really I am.

EDIE: What, then?

DON: I just wanted to say. In case we don't...you know. Meet.

EDIE: I've said we will.

DON: But we don't know. Do we?

EDIE: No.

DON: So I wanted to say. Sometimes. When I couldn't sleep nights, I'd look across at you, in your frilly nighty. And I'd think, by 'eck lad. You're a jammy bugger. How did you manage that?

EDIE: (*Thrilled.*) Did you?

DON: You know what makes this alright? We took every moment and wrung it out for all it was worth. Every second. Every touch. Every share. My life would've been worthless without you, Edie. If I hadn't met you, it wouldn't've been worth being here. You're the greatest woman ever walked God's earth. No word of a lie.

EDIE: We've been lucky to find each other. Imagine if I'd been late that night. Imagine missing you by a beat. Imagine not finding you. I wouldn't have liked that. I love you, Don.

DON: I love you, Edie. It's time, isn't it?

EDIE: Say goodnight Gracie.

DON: Goodnight Gracie.

DON goes over to the chair. Sits.

EDIE holds the equipment. She walks slowly over to DON. As she does so, the lights fade. Cross fade to the fire escape steps. TONY and RUTH are climbing up to the roof. RUTH is intrepidly leading the way. TONY is still clasping DON and EDIE's bottle of champagne.

TONY: Ruth!

RUTH: Just keep good hold of that champagne.

They clamber on to the roof. Sit and look out. The sun is beginning to rise. They bask in the orange glow. All we can hear is the night air. Loud and thick and silent.

TONY: Wow.

RUTH: It's gorgeous up here.

TONY: Sun's starting to come up in full.

The light envelopes them further.

TONY: It's so quiet.

RUTH: Maybe the party's finished.

TONY: (*Looking down.*) Look!

RUTH: What?

TONY: The flowers.

RUTH: Oh yeah.

TONY: Didn't do a bad job, did we?

They smile.

RUTH: I've made a decision. About Neil and you and… me. Mostly about me.

TONY: Oh. Right. Fine. How are you? Alright?

RUTH: D'you want to know?

TONY: Course I bloody do!

RUTH: Well. I think you're –

TONY: (*Listening.*) Hang on a sec!

RUTH: (*Indignant.*) Do you always have to interrupt? I'm trying to –

TONY: Ssh! Wait a sec. Listen!

RUTH: What?

TONY: Can you hear that?

They both listen. From the floor below, we hear EDIE singing. A lone voice. She sings 'Just One Look'.

We see nothing but RUTH and TONY.

EDIE continues to sing unseen. Her voice is faltering with sorrow and love. We hear her voice crack and break and falter.

RUTH and TONY sit there for a moment.

You were saying?

RUTH: Sorry?

TONY: You were going to say something.

RUTH: Oh. Shall we open the champagne?

They look at each other.

TONY: Why don't we save it? For a rainy day.

RUTH: Yeah. Let's save it.

Beat.

Will you do something for me?

TONY: What?

They look at each other.

Kiss. A perfect beautiful first kiss.

Delicate. Linger.

RUTH: Yeah.

They look out.

From the floor below, 'Long After This Night Is All Over' by Jimmy Radcliffe begins to play.

TONY and RUTH stay looking out. They hold hands. Smiles spread slowly across their faces.

As the chorus hits, snap black out. Music comes up, loud.

The End.

Author's Note
(Where to find the music)

Act One
Sex Bomb – Tom Jones with Mousse T
from Tom Jones: Reload GUTCD009

Don't Falter – Mint Royale
from Mint Royale: On The Ropes FHCD011

Act Two
Just One Look – Doris Troy
from At The Club (compilation) CDKEND 168

Que Sera, Sera (Whatever Will Be, Will Be) – The High
Keys
from At The Club (compilation) CDKEND 168

Long After Tonight Is All Over – Jimmy Radcliffe
*from Cooler Shakers! 30 Northern Soul Floorstompers
(compilation) MCCD319*

*The title of play is a reference to a couple of sources, the most obvi-
ous of which is the song of the same name by The Magnetic Fields
on their (fantastic) CD, 69 Love Songs.*

Chris Chibnall
London, 2001

By the same author

Worst Wedding Ever
9781783191024

WWW.OBERONBOOKS.COM

Follow us on www.twitter.com/@oberonbooks
& www.facebook.com/OberonBooksLondon